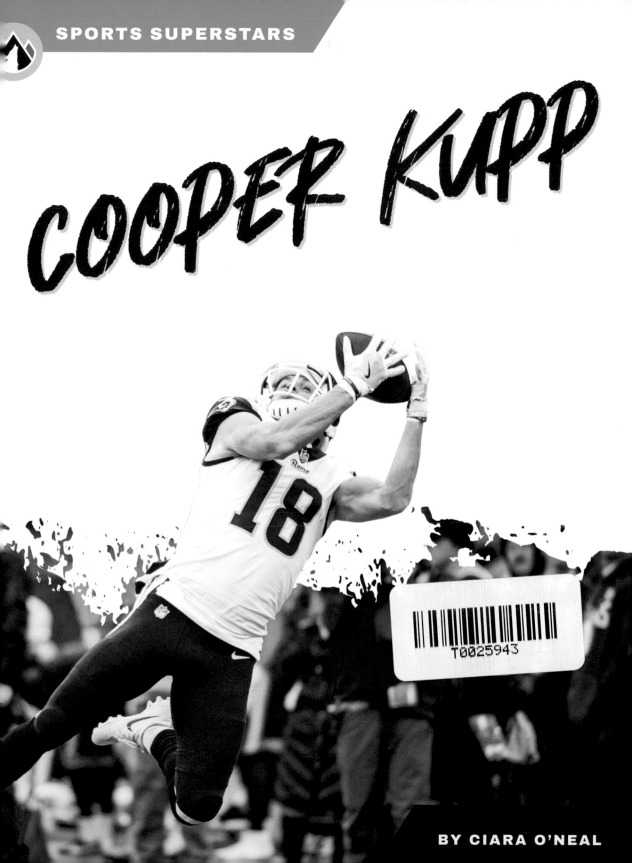

COOPER KUPP

T0025943

BY CIARA O'NEAL

Apex is distributed by North Star Editions:
sales@northstareditions.com | 888-417-0195

Produced for Apex by Red Line Editorial.

Photographs ©: Ben Liebenberg/AP Images, cover; Austin Anthony/Daily News/AP Images, 1, 16–17; Ric Tapia/AP Images, 4–5, 7; Adam Hunger/AP Images, 8; Jeff Bukowski/Shutterstock Images, 9, 19, 29; Real Window Creative/Shutterstock Images, 10–11; Robert Johnson/SPTSW/ AP Images, 13; Adrian Sanchez-Gonzales/The Daily Chronicle/AP Images, 14–15; Ryan Kang/ AP Images, 18, 20–21; Jason Behnken/AP Images, 22–23; Elliott Cowand Jr./Shutterstock Images, 24–25; Steve Luciano/AP Images, 27

Library of Congress Control Number: 2022922224

ISBN
978-1-63738-557-9 (hardcover)
978-1-63738-611-8 (paperback)
978-1-63738-715-3 (ebook pdf)
978-1-63738-665-1 (hosted ebook)

Printed in the United States of America
Mankato, MN
082023

NOTE TO PARENTS AND EDUCATORS

Apex books are designed to build literacy skills in striving readers. Exciting, high-interest content attracts and holds readers' attention. The text is carefully leveled to allow students to achieve success quickly. Additional features, such as bolded glossary words for difficult terms, help build comprehension.

TABLE OF CONTENTS

CHAPTER 1

KUPP FOR THE WIN

Super Bowl LVI is almost over. The Los Angeles Rams are down by four points. But the end zone is just one yard away.

Super Bowl LVI took place on February 13, 2022. The Los Angeles Rams played the Cincinnati Bengals.

The Rams snap the ball to their quarterback, Matthew Stafford. He spots Cooper Kupp darting toward the end zone. A **defender** closes in. But Kupp runs fast to break free.

FAST FACT

Kupp plays wide receiver. It's his job to catch the quarterback's passes.

Kupp runs to get open for a pass during the Super Bowl.

Stafford throws the ball. Kupp grabs it out of the air. It's a touchdown! The Rams win the game, 23–20.

Kupp makes a touchdown catch in the second half of Super Bowl LVI.

Every year, the winner of
the Super Bowl MVP
Award gets a trophy.

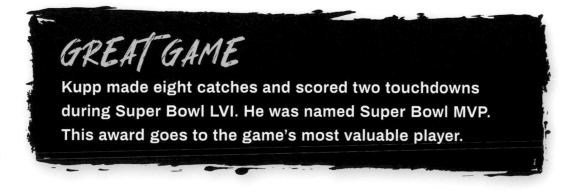

GREAT GAME

Kupp made eight catches and scored two touchdowns
during Super Bowl LVI. He was named Super Bowl MVP.
This award goes to the game's most valuable player.

CHAPTER 2

A RISING STAR

Cooper Kupp grew up in Yakima, Washington. He played basketball and football in high school. He was an All-State athlete in football.

Kupp was born and raised in Yakima, Washington.

However, Kupp was small and thin. So, few colleges paid attention to him. One that did was Eastern Washington University. Kupp got a **scholarship** to play football there.

FAMILY TIES

Kupp has three siblings. They played sports, too. Both his brothers played football. His sister played soccer. All of them went to Eastern Washington University.

Kupp scores a touchdown for the Eastern Washington Eagles.

In 2015, Kupp was named the best **offensive** player in his **division**.

Kupp makes a catch during a game against Montana State.

Kupp quickly showed his skills. He set records for catches and touchdowns. When he left college, he had the most **receiving yards** in the history of college football.

CHAPTER 3

GOING PRO

Kupp was ready for the NFL. The Los Angeles Rams chose him in the 2017 **draft**. He scored a touchdown in the first game of the year.

Kupp scored five touchdowns during his first NFL season.

In 2018, Kupp hurt his knee. He missed the end of the season and the **playoffs**. But he didn't let the injury stop him.

The Rams reached the Super Bowl after the 2018 season. But they lost to the New England Patriots.

Kupp's grandpa, Jake, played in the NFL from 1964 to 1975.

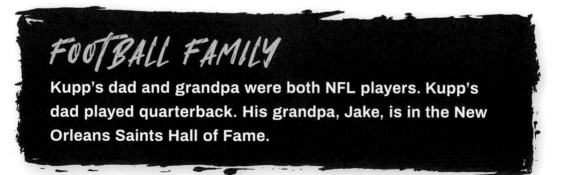

FOOTBALL FAMILY

Kupp's dad and grandpa were both NFL players. Kupp's dad played quarterback. His grandpa, Jake, is in the New Orleans Saints Hall of Fame.

Kupp made a huge comeback in 2019. He worked hard and became faster than ever. That season, he caught more than 90 passes.

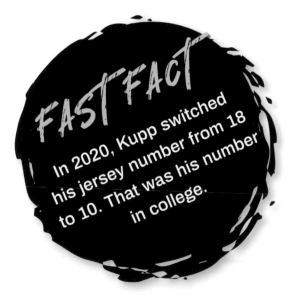

FAST FACT

In 2020, Kupp switched his jersey number from 18 to 10. That was his number in college.

Kupp dodges a defender during a 2019 game against the Arizona Cardinals.

CHAPTER 4

NFL CHAMP

In 2021, Kupp had his best season yet. He led the Rams back to the playoffs. They even reached the Super Bowl.

Matthew Stafford (9) and Kupp (10) connected for 145 catches during the 2021 season.

Super Bowl LVI took place at the Rams' home stadium near Los Angeles, California.

Super Bowl LVI was a close game. The Rams faced the Cincinnati Bengals. Kupp's two touchdown catches helped his team win.

FAST FACT

Kupp had 1,947 yards in the 2021 season. He added 478 more during the playoffs.

Kupp was named Offensive Player of the Year. In 2022, he signed a new **contract** with the Rams. Fans looked forward to even more great plays.

TRIPLE CROWN

Kupp won the receiving triple crown after the 2021 season. That means he led the NFL in three stats. These stats are total catches, receiving yards, and touchdown catches.

Kupp celebrates after winning the Super Bowl.

COMPREHENSION QUESTIONS

Write your answers on a separate piece of paper.

1. Write a few sentences describing the main ideas of Chapter 2.

2. Which of Kupp's awards do you think is most impressive? Why?

3. Which position does Kupp play?

    A. defender

    B. quarterback

    C. wide receiver

4. Why would college football teams be less interested in small, thin players?

    A. Smaller players are often faster and stronger.

    B. Smaller players are often slower and weaker.

    C. Smaller players rarely get hurt.

5. What does **athlete** mean in this book?

He played basketball and football in high school.
*He was an All-State **athlete** in football.*

    A. a person who plays sports
    B. a person who cooks food
    C. a person who attends college

6. What does **comeback** mean in this book?

*Kupp made a huge **comeback** in 2019. He*
worked hard and became faster than ever.

    A. a return to success
    B. a series of losses
    C. a big problem

Answer key on page 32.

GLOSSARY

contract
An agreement to pay someone money, often for doing work.

defender
A player who tries to stop the other team from scoring.

division
A group of teams within a league.

draft
A system where professional teams choose new players.

offensive
Related to the team or players who are trying to score.

playoffs
A set of games played after the regular season to decide which team will be the champion.

receiving yards
The number of yards gained by a receiver on a passing play.

scholarship
Money given to someone to help pay for college.

TO LEARN MORE

BOOKS

Abdo, Kenny. *Los Angeles Rams.* Minneapolis: Abdo Publishing, 2022.

Coleman, Ted. *Los Angeles Rams All-Time Greats.* Mendota Heights, MN: Press Box Books, 2022.

Mitchell, Bo. *The Super Bowl.* Mendota Heights, MN: Apex Editions, 2023.

ONLINE RESOURCES

Visit **www.apexeditions.com** to find links and resources related to this title.

ABOUT THE AUTHOR

Ciara O'Neal is a proud author and mama. This book is for AJ, who inspires her to try new things.

INDEX

ANSWER KEY:
1. Answers will vary; 2. Answers will vary; 3. C; 4. B; 5. A; 6. A